NEW INTERNATIONAL VERSION

# NIV
# Beautiful
# WORD™
## BIBLE JOURNAL

•

# Proverbs

**ZONDERVAN®**

*NIV Beautiful Word™ Bible Journal, Proverbs*
Published by Zondervan, 2021
Grand Rapids, Michigan, USA
All rights reserved

www.Zondervan.com

This Bible was set in the Zondervan NIV Typeface, created at the 2K/DENMARK type foundry.

Any Internet addresses (websites, blogs, etc.) and telephone numbers in this Bible are offered as a resource. They are not intended in any way to be or imply an endorsement by Zondervan, nor does Zondervan vouch for the content of these sites and numbers for the life of the Bible.

*Printed in China*

N120712

21 22 23 24 25 26 /AMC/ 15 14 13 12 11 10 9 8 7 6 5 4 3 2 1

A portion of the purchase price of your NIV® Bible is provided to Biblica so together we support the mission of *Transforming lives through God's Word.*

Biblica provides God's Word to people through translation, publishing and Bible engagement in Africa, Asia Pacific, Europe, Latin America, Middle East, and North America. Through its worldwide reach, Biblica engages people with God's Word so that their lives are transformed through a relationship with Jesus Christ.

# Table of Contents

# Letter from the Editor

*"Beautiful words, wonderful words, wonderful words of life."*

The closing line of Philip P. Bliss's hymn says it perfectly. God's Word is filled with beautiful, wonderful words that give us life. The words of Scripture are indeed beautiful for their love, grace, exhortation, correction, wisdom, hope and truth. While we know that God's Word stands alone and needs no help from us to speak to the reader, in this Bible we complemented Scripture with illustrations of God's beautiful words. In partnership with nine unique artists who each brought their own personal creative style to 600 verses, we added visual beauty to the pages of Scripture.

With the help from data collected by BibleGateway, we selected key verses that online Bible readers search most often. We paired our review with an editorial eye to select verses that represented every book of the Bible and that balanced popular verses with less familiar ones. Some verses are great to memorize; others will introduce you to a section of God's Word that may be unfamiliar.

We hope that through the beauty of these illustrated words, you will pause, read and be drawn in to explore God's Word deeper than you have before. We also hope that the artwork will inspire you to illustrate or journal about your favorite, life-changing verses and passages in the margins of this special journal edition.

We pray that this inspirational, Scripture-based art will open your heart to his beautiful, wonderful words of life in a way you've never experienced.

Melinda Bouma
*Publisher, Zondervan Bible Group*

# Tips for Bible Art Journaling

**Use the right pen** — Look for a pen designed for Bible journaling to minimize bleed through and tears. There are many options available in a rainbow of colors. Or, try your hand at colored pencils for a great alternative to pens.

**Practice on scrap paper** — Learn key factors like spacing and ink-drying time before you make your mark on your Bible.

**Use back pages** — Try out your art on the pages in the back of this Bible Journal to help build your confidence.

**Integrate washi tape** — Just a little tape under favorite verses and around the edge adds a lot of interest to the pages.

**Peel and stick** — You name it, there is a sticker for it: from letters and pictures, to shapes, ribbons, and designs. You don't have to be an accomplished artist to brighten your pages with stickers.

**Stencil and stamp** — Just like stickers, there are endless options in these categories to enhance your Bible without having an art degree.

**Get inspired** — Reflect on the designs found in the *NIV Beautiful Word™ Bible* or on your favorite verse art to help spark ideas.

**Don't stress about mistakes** — You will make them, but just learn from them and let go of perfectionism!

# Preface

The goal of the New International Version (NIV) is to enable English-speaking people from around the world to read and hear God's eternal Word in their own language. Our work as translators is motivated by our conviction that the Bible is God's Word in written form. We believe that the Bible contains the divine answer to the deepest needs of humanity, sheds unique light on our path in a dark world and sets forth the way to our eternal well-being. Out of these deep convictions, we have sought to recreate as far as possible the experience of the original audience — blending transparency to the original text with accessibility for the millions of English speakers around the world. We have prioritized accuracy, clarity and literary quality with the goal of creating a translation suitable for public and private reading, evangelism, teaching, preaching, memorizing and liturgical use. We have also sought to preserve a measure of continuity with the long tradition of translating the Scriptures into English.

The complete NIV Bible was first published in 1978. It was a completely new translation made by over a hundred scholars working directly from the best available Hebrew, Aramaic and Greek texts. The translators came from the United States, Great Britain, Canada, Australia and New Zealand, giving the translation an international scope. They were from many denominations and churches — including Anglican, Assemblies of God, Baptist, Brethren, Christian Reformed, Church of Christ, Evangelical Covenant, Evangelical Free, Lutheran, Mennonite, Methodist, Nazarene, Presbyterian, Wesleyan and others. This breadth of denominational and theological perspective helped to safeguard the translation from sectarian bias. For these reasons, and by the grace of God, the NIV has gained a wide readership in all parts of the English-speaking world.

The work of translating the Bible is never finished. As good as they are, English translations must be regularly updated so that they will continue to communicate accurately the meaning of God's Word. Updates are needed in order to reflect the latest developments in our understanding of the biblical world and its languages and to keep pace with changes in English usage. Recognizing, then, that the NIV would retain its ability to communicate God's Word accurately only if it were regularly updated, the original translators established the Committee on Bible Translation (CBT). The Committee is a self-perpetuating group of biblical scholars charged with keeping abreast of advances in biblical scholarship and changes in English and issuing periodic updates to the NIV. The CBT is an independent, self-governing body and has sole responsibility for the NIV text. The Committee mirrors the original group of translators in its diverse international and denominational makeup and in its unifying commitment to the Bible as God's inspired Word.

In obedience to its mandate, the Committee has issued periodic updates to the NIV. An initial revision was released in 1984. A more thorough revision process was completed in 2005, resulting in the separately published TNIV. The updated NIV you now have in your hands builds on both the original NIV and the TNIV and represents the latest effort of the Committee to articulate God's unchanging Word in the way the original authors might have said it had they been speaking in English to the global English-speaking audience today.

## Translation Philosophy

The Committee's translating work has been governed by three widely accepted principles about the way people use words and about the way we understand them.

First, the meaning of words is determined by the way that users of the language actually use them at any given time. For the biblical languages, therefore, the Committee utilizes the best and most recent scholarship on the way Hebrew, Aramaic and Greek words were being used in biblical times. At the same time, the Committee carefully studies the state of modern English. Good translation is like good communication: one must know the target audience so that the appropriate choices can be made about which English words to use to represent the original words of Scripture. From its inception, the NIV has had as its target the general English-speaking population all over the world, the "International" in its title reflecting this concern. The aim of the Committee is to put the Scriptures into natural English that will communicate effectively with the broadest possible audience of English speakers.

Modern technology has enhanced the Committee's ability to choose the right English words to convey the meaning of the original text. The field of computational linguistics harnesses the power of computers to provide broadly applicable and current data about the state of the language. Translators can now access huge databases of modern English to better understand the current meaning and usage of key words.

The Committee utilized this resource in preparing the 2011 edition of the NIV. An area of especially rapid and significant change in English is the way certain nouns and pronouns are used to refer to human beings. The Committee therefore requested experts in computational linguistics at Collins Dictionaries to pose some key questions about this usage to its database of English — the largest in the world, with over 4.4 billion words, gathered from several English-speaking countries and including both spoken and written English. (The Collins Study, called "The Development and Use of Gender Language in Contemporary English," can be accessed at *http://www.thenivbible.com/about-the-niv/about-the-2011-edition/*.) The study revealed that the most popular words to describe the human race in modern U.S. English were "humanity," "man" and "mankind." The Committee then used this data in the updated NIV, choosing from among these three words (and occasionally others also) depending on the context.

A related issue creates a larger problem for modern translations: the move away from using the third-person masculine singular pronouns — "he/him/his" — to refer to men and women equally. This usage does persist in some forms of English, and this revision therefore occasionally uses these pronouns in a generic sense. But the tendency, recognized in day-to-day usage and confirmed by the Collins study, is away from the generic use of "he," "him" and "his." In recognition of this shift in language and in an effort to translate into the natural English that people are actually using, this revision of the NIV generally uses other constructions when the biblical text is plainly addressed to men and women equally. The reader will encounter especially frequently a "they," "their" or "them" to express a generic singular idea. Thus, for instance, Mark 8:36 reads: "What good is it for someone to gain the whole world, yet forfeit their soul?" This generic use of the "distributive" or "singular" "they/them/their" has been used for many centuries by respected writers of English and has now become established as standard English, spoken and written, all over the world.

A second linguistic principle that feeds into the Committee's translation work is that meaning is found not in individual words, as vital as they are, but in larger clusters: phrases, clauses, sentences, discourses. Translation is not, as many people think, a matter of word substitution: English word *x* in place of Hebrew word *y*. Translators must first determine the meaning of the words of the biblical languages in the context of the passage and then select English words that accurately communicate that meaning to modern listeners and readers. This means that accurate translation will not always reflect the exact structure of the original language. To be sure, there is debate over the degree to which translators should try to preserve the "form" of the original text in English. From the beginning, the NIV has taken a mediating position on this issue. The manual produced when the translation that became the NIV was first being planned states: "If the Greek or Hebrew syntax has a good parallel in modern English, it should be used. But if there is no good parallel, the English syntax appropriate to the meaning of the original is to be chosen." It is fine, in other words, to carry over the form of the biblical languages into English — but not at the expense of natural expression. The principle that meaning resides in larger clusters of words means that the Committee has not insisted on a "word-for-word" approach to translation. We certainly believe that every word of Scripture is inspired by God and therefore to be carefully studied to determine what God is saying to us. It is for this reason that the Committee labors over every single word of the original texts, working hard to determine how each of those words contributes to what the text is saying. Ultimately, however, it is how these individual words function in combination with other words that determines meaning.

A third linguistic principle guiding the Committee in its translation work is the recognition that words have a spectrum of meaning. It is popular to define a word by using another word, or "gloss," to substitute for it. This substitute word is then sometimes called the "literal" meaning of a word. In fact, however, words have a range of possible meanings. Those meanings will vary depending on the context, and words in one language will usually not occupy the same semantic range as words in another language. The Committee therefore studies each original word of Scripture in its context to identify its meaning in a particular verse and then chooses an appropriate English word (or phrase) to represent it. It is impossible, then, to translate any given Hebrew, Aramaic or Greek word with the same English word all the time. The Committee does try to translate related occurrences of a word in the original languages with the same English word in order to preserve the connection for the English reader. But the Committee generally privileges clear natural meaning over a concern with consistency in rendering particular words.

## Textual Basis

For the Old Testament the standard Hebrew text, the Masoretic Text as published in the latest edition of *Biblia Hebraica*, has been used throughout. The Masoretic Text tradition contains marginal notations that offer variant readings. These have sometimes been followed instead of the text itself. Because such instances involve variants within the Masoretic tradition, they have not been indicated in the textual notes. In a few cases, words in the basic consonantal text have been divided differently than in the Masoretic Text. Such cases are usually indicated in the textual footnotes. The Dead Sea Scrolls contain biblical texts that represent an earlier stage of the transmission of the Hebrew text. They have been consulted, as have been the Samaritan Pentateuch and the ancient scribal traditions concerning deliberate textual changes. The translators also consulted the more important early versions. Readings from these versions, the Dead Sea Scrolls and the scribal traditions were occasionally followed where the Masoretic Text seemed doubtful and where accepted principles of textual criticism showed that one or more of these textual witnesses appeared to provide the correct reading. In rare cases, the translators have emended the Hebrew text where it appears to have become corrupted at an even earlier stage of its transmission. These departures from the Masoretic Text are also indicated in the textual footnotes. Sometimes the vowel indicators (which are later additions to the basic consonantal text) found in the Masoretic Text did not, in the judgment of the translators, represent the correct vowels for the original text. Accordingly, some words have been read with a different set of vowels. These instances are usually not indicated in the footnotes.

The Greek text used in translating the New Testament has been an eclectic one, based on the latest editions of the Nestle-Aland/United Bible Societies' Greek New Testament. The translators have made their choices among the variant readings in accordance with widely accepted principles of New Testament textual criticism. Footnotes call attention to places where uncertainty remains.

The New Testament authors, writing in Greek, often quote the Old Testament from its ancient Greek version, the Septuagint. This is one reason why some of the Old Testament quotations in the NIV New Testament are not identical to the corresponding passages in the NIV Old Testament. Such quotations in the New Testament are indicated with the footnote "(see Septuagint)."

## Footnotes and Formatting

Footnotes in this version are of several kinds, most of which need no explanation. Those giving alternative translations begin with "Or" and generally introduce the alternative with the last word preceding it in the text, except when it is a single-word alternative. When poetry is quoted in a footnote a slash mark indicates a line division.

It should be noted that references to diseases, minerals, flora and fauna, architectural details, clothing, jewelry, musical instru-

ments and other articles cannot always be identified with precision. Also, linear measurements and measures of capacity can only be approximated (see the Table of Weights and Measures). Although *Selah*, used mainly in the Psalms, is probably a musical term, its meaning is uncertain. Since it may interrupt reading and distract the reader, this word has not been kept in the English text, but every occurrence has been signaled by a footnote.

As an aid to the reader, sectional headings have been inserted. They are not to be regarded as part of the biblical text and are not intended for oral reading. It is the Committee's hope that these headings may prove more helpful to the reader than the traditional chapter divisions, which were introduced long after the Bible was written.

Sometimes the chapter and/or verse numbering in English translations of the Old Testament differs from that found in published Hebrew texts. This is particularly the case in the Psalms, where the traditional titles are included in the Hebrew verse numbering. Such differences are indicated in the footnotes at the bottom of the page. In the New Testament, verse numbers that marked off portions of the traditional English text not supported by the best Greek manuscripts now appear in brackets, with a footnote indicating the text that has been omitted (see, for example, Matthew 17:[21]).

Mark 16:9 – 20 and John 7:53 — 8:11, although long accorded virtually equal status with the rest of the Gospels in which they stand, have a questionable standing in the textual history of the New Testament, as noted in the bracketed annotations with which they are set off. A different typeface has been chosen for these passages to indicate their uncertain status.

Basic formatting of the text, such as lining the poetry, paragraphing (both prose and poetry), setting up of (administrative-like) lists, indenting letters and lengthy prayers within narratives and the insertion of sectional headings, has been the work of the Committee. However, the choice between single-column and double-column formats has been left to the publishers. Also the issuing of "red-letter" editions is a publisher's choice — one that the Committee does not endorse.

The Committee has again been reminded that every human effort is flawed — including this revision of the NIV. We trust, however, that many will find in it an improved representation of the Word of God, through which they hear his call to faith in our Lord Jesus Christ and to service in his kingdom. We offer this version of the Bible to him in whose name and for whose glory it has been made.

The Committee on Bible Translation

# Proverbs

## Purpose and Theme

**1** The proverbs of Solomon son of David, king of Israel:

<sup>2</sup> for gaining wisdom and instruction;
  for understanding words of insight;
<sup>3</sup> for receiving instruction in prudent behavior,
  doing what is right and just and fair;
<sup>4</sup> for giving prudence to those who are simple,[a]
  knowledge and discretion to the young —
<sup>5</sup> let the wise listen and add to their learning,
  and let the discerning get guidance —
<sup>6</sup> for understanding proverbs and parables,
  the sayings and riddles of the wise.[b]

<sup>7</sup> The fear of the LORD is the beginning of knowledge,
  but fools[c] despise wisdom and instruction.

## Prologue: Exhortations to Embrace Wisdom

### Warning Against the Invitation of Sinful Men

<sup>8</sup> Listen, my son, to your father's instruction
  and do not forsake your mother's teaching.
<sup>9</sup> They are a garland to grace your head
  and a chain to adorn your neck.

<sup>10</sup> My son, if sinful men entice you,
  do not give in to them.
<sup>11</sup> If they say, "Come along with us;
  let's lie in wait for innocent blood,
  let's ambush some harmless soul;
<sup>12</sup> let's swallow them alive, like the grave,
  and whole, like those who go down to the pit;
<sup>13</sup> we will get all sorts of valuable things
  and fill our houses with plunder;
<sup>14</sup> cast lots with us;
  we will all share the loot" —
<sup>15</sup> my son, do not go along with them,
  do not set foot on their paths;
<sup>16</sup> for their feet rush into evil,
  they are swift to shed blood.
<sup>17</sup> How useless to spread a net
  where every bird can see it!

---

[a] 4 The Hebrew word rendered *simple* in Proverbs denotes a person who is gullible, without moral direction and inclined to evil.    [b] 6 Or *understanding a proverb, namely, a parable, / and the sayings of the wise, their riddles*    [c] 7 The Hebrew words rendered *fool* in Proverbs, and often elsewhere in the Old Testament, denote a person who is morally deficient.

the fear
of the
LORD
is the
beginning
of
knowledge,
but fools
despise
wisdom
and
instruction.

PROVERBS 1:7

<sup>18</sup> These men lie in wait for their own blood;
    they ambush only themselves!
<sup>19</sup> Such are the paths of all who go after ill-gotten gain;
    it takes away the life of those who get it.

## Wisdom's Rebuke

<sup>20</sup> Out in the open wisdom calls aloud,
    she raises her voice in the public square;
<sup>21</sup> on top of the wall<sup>a</sup> she cries out,
    at the city gate she makes her speech:

<sup>22</sup> "How long will you who are simple love your simple ways?
    How long will mockers delight in mockery
    and fools hate knowledge?
<sup>23</sup> Repent at my rebuke!
    Then I will pour out my thoughts to you,
    I will make known to you my teachings.
<sup>24</sup> But since you refuse to listen when I call
    and no one pays attention when I stretch out my hand,
<sup>25</sup> since you disregard all my advice
    and do not accept my rebuke,
<sup>26</sup> I in turn will laugh when disaster strikes you;
    I will mock when calamity overtakes you —
<sup>27</sup> when calamity overtakes you like a storm,
    when disaster sweeps over you like a whirlwind,
    when distress and trouble overwhelm you.

<sup>28</sup> "Then they will call to me but I will not answer;
    they will look for me but will not find me,
<sup>29</sup> since they hated knowledge
    and did not choose to fear the LORD.
<sup>30</sup> Since they would not accept my advice
    and spurned my rebuke,
<sup>31</sup> they will eat the fruit of their ways
    and be filled with the fruit of their schemes.
<sup>32</sup> For the waywardness of the simple will kill them,
    and the complacency of fools will destroy them;
<sup>33</sup> but whoever listens to me will live in safety
    and be at ease, without fear of harm."

## Moral Benefits of Wisdom

**2** My son, if you accept my words
    and store up my commands within you,
<sup>2</sup> turning your ear to wisdom
    and applying your heart to understanding —
<sup>3</sup> indeed, if you call out for insight
    and cry aloud for understanding,
<sup>4</sup> and if you look for it as for silver
    and search for it as for hidden treasure,
<sup>5</sup> then you will understand the fear of the LORD
    and find the knowledge of God.
<sup>6</sup> For the LORD gives wisdom;
    from his mouth come knowledge and understanding.

---

<sup>a</sup> *21* Septuagint; Hebrew / *at noisy street corners*

⁷ He holds success in store for the upright,
    he is a shield to those whose walk is blameless,
⁸ for he guards the course of the just
    and protects the way of his faithful ones.

⁹ Then you will understand what is right and just
    and fair — every good path.
¹⁰ For wisdom will enter your heart,
    and knowledge will be pleasant to your soul.
¹¹ Discretion will protect you,
    and understanding will guard you.

¹² Wisdom will save you from the ways of wicked men,
    from men whose words are perverse,
¹³ who have left the straight paths
    to walk in dark ways,
¹⁴ who delight in doing wrong
    and rejoice in the perverseness of evil,
¹⁵ whose paths are crooked
    and who are devious in their ways.

¹⁶ Wisdom will save you also from the adulterous woman,
    from the wayward woman with her seductive words,
¹⁷ who has left the partner of her youth
    and ignored the covenant she made before God.ᵃ
¹⁸ Surely her house leads down to death
    and her paths to the spirits of the dead.
¹⁹ None who go to her return
    or attain the paths of life.

²⁰ Thus you will walk in the ways of the good
    and keep to the paths of the righteous.
²¹ For the upright will live in the land,
    and the blameless will remain in it;
²² but the wicked will be cut off from the land,
    and the unfaithful will be torn from it.

## Wisdom Bestows Well-Being

**3** My son, do not forget my teaching,
    but keep my commands in your heart,
² for they will prolong your life many years
    and bring you peace and prosperity.

³ Let love and faithfulness never leave you;
    bind them around your neck,
    write them on the tablet of your heart.
⁴ Then you will win favor and a good name
    in the sight of God and man.

⁵ Trust in the LORD with all your heart
    and lean not on your own understanding;
⁶ in all your ways submit to him,
    and he will make your paths straight.ᵇ

⁷ Do not be wise in your own eyes;
    fear the LORD and shun evil.

ᵃ 17 Or *covenant of her God*    ᵇ 6 Or *will direct your paths*

8 This will bring health to your body
   and nourishment to your bones.

9 Honor the LORD with your wealth,
   with the firstfruits of all your crops;
10 then your barns will be filled to overflowing,
   and your vats will brim over with new wine.

11 My son, do not despise the LORD's discipline,
   and do not resent his rebuke,
12 because the LORD disciplines those he loves,
   as a father the son he delights in.*a*

13 Blessed are those who find wisdom,
   those who gain understanding,
14 for she is more profitable than silver
   and yields better returns than gold.
15 She is more precious than rubies;
   nothing you desire can compare with her.
16 Long life is in her right hand;
   in her left hand are riches and honor.
17 Her ways are pleasant ways,
   and all her paths are peace.
18 She is a tree of life to those who take hold of her;
   those who hold her fast will be blessed.

19 By wisdom the LORD laid the earth's foundations,
   by understanding he set the heavens in place;
20 by his knowledge the watery depths were divided,
   and the clouds let drop the dew.

21 My son, do not let wisdom and understanding out of your sight,
   preserve sound judgment and discretion;
22 they will be life for you,
   an ornament to grace your neck.
23 Then you will go on your way in safety,
   and your foot will not stumble.
24 When you lie down, you will not be afraid;
   when you lie down, your sleep will be sweet.
25 Have no fear of sudden disaster
   or of the ruin that overtakes the wicked,
26 for the LORD will be at your side
   and will keep your foot from being snared.

27 Do not withhold good from those to whom it is due,
   when it is in your power to act.
28 Do not say to your neighbor,
   "Come back tomorrow and I'll give it to you" —
   when you already have it with you.
29 Do not plot harm against your neighbor,
   who lives trustfully near you.
30 Do not accuse anyone for no reason —
   when they have done you no harm.

31 Do not envy the violent
   or choose any of their ways.

---

*a* 12 Hebrew; Septuagint *loves, / and he chastens everyone he accepts as his child*

Do not withhold good from those to whom it is due, when it is in your power to act.
PROVERBS 3:27

³² For the Lord detests the perverse
     but takes the upright into his confidence.
³³ The Lord's curse is on the house of the wicked,
     but he blesses the home of the righteous.
³⁴ He mocks proud mockers
     but shows favor to the humble and oppressed.
³⁵ The wise inherit honor,
     but fools get only shame.

## Get Wisdom at Any Cost

4 Listen, my sons, to a father's instruction;
     pay attention and gain understanding.
² I give you sound learning,
     so do not forsake my teaching.
³ For I too was a son to my father,
     still tender, and cherished by my mother.
⁴ Then he taught me, and he said to me,
     "Take hold of my words with all your heart;
     keep my commands, and you will live.
⁵ Get wisdom, get understanding;
     do not forget my words or turn away from them.
⁶ Do not forsake wisdom, and she will protect you;
     love her, and she will watch over you.
⁷ The beginning of wisdom is this: Get^a wisdom.
     Though it cost all you have,^b get understanding.
⁸ Cherish her, and she will exalt you;
     embrace her, and she will honor you.
⁹ She will give you a garland to grace your head
     and present you with a glorious crown."

¹⁰ Listen, my son, accept what I say,
     and the years of your life will be many.
¹¹ I instruct you in the way of wisdom
     and lead you along straight paths.
¹² When you walk, your steps will not be hampered;
     when you run, you will not stumble.
¹³ Hold on to instruction, do not let it go;
     guard it well, for it is your life.
¹⁴ Do not set foot on the path of the wicked
     or walk in the way of evildoers.
¹⁵ Avoid it, do not travel on it;
     turn from it and go on your way.
¹⁶ For they cannot rest until they do evil;
     they are robbed of sleep till they make someone stumble.
¹⁷ They eat the bread of wickedness
     and drink the wine of violence.

¹⁸ The path of the righteous is like the morning sun,
     shining ever brighter till the full light of day.
¹⁹ But the way of the wicked is like deep darkness;
     they do not know what makes them stumble.

²⁰ My son, pay attention to what I say;
     turn your ear to my words.

---

^a 7 Or *Wisdom is supreme; therefore get*     ^b 7 Or *wisdom. / Whatever else you get*

²¹ Do not let them out of your sight,
 keep them within your heart;
²² for they are life to those who find them
 and health to one's whole body.
²³ Above all else, guard your heart,
 for everything you do flows from it.
²⁴ Keep your mouth free of perversity;
 keep corrupt talk far from your lips.
²⁵ Let your eyes look straight ahead;
 fix your gaze directly before you.
²⁶ Give careful thought to the[a] paths for your feet
 and be steadfast in all your ways.
²⁷ Do not turn to the right or the left;
 keep your foot from evil.

## Warning Against Adultery

**5** My son, pay attention to my wisdom,
 turn your ear to my words of insight,
² that you may maintain discretion
 and your lips may preserve knowledge.
³ For the lips of the adulterous woman drip honey,
 and her speech is smoother than oil;
⁴ but in the end she is bitter as gall,
 sharp as a double-edged sword.
⁵ Her feet go down to death;
 her steps lead straight to the grave.
⁶ She gives no thought to the way of life;
 her paths wander aimlessly, but she does not know it.

⁷ Now then, my sons, listen to me;
 do not turn aside from what I say.
⁸ Keep to a path far from her,
 do not go near the door of her house,
⁹ lest you lose your honor to others
 and your dignity[b] to one who is cruel,
¹⁰ lest strangers feast on your wealth
 and your toil enrich the house of another.
¹¹ At the end of your life you will groan,
 when your flesh and body are spent.
¹² You will say, "How I hated discipline!
 How my heart spurned correction!
¹³ I would not obey my teachers
 or turn my ear to my instructors.
¹⁴ And I was soon in serious trouble
 in the assembly of God's people."

¹⁵ Drink water from your own cistern,
 running water from your own well.
¹⁶ Should your springs overflow in the streets,
 your streams of water in the public squares?
¹⁷ Let them be yours alone,
 never to be shared with strangers.
¹⁸ May your fountain be blessed,
 and may you rejoice in the wife of your youth.

---

[a] 26 Or *Make level*  [b] 9 Or *years*

¹⁹ A loving doe, a graceful deer —
    may her breasts satisfy you always,
    may you ever be intoxicated with her love.
²⁰ Why, my son, be intoxicated with another man's wife?
    Why embrace the bosom of a wayward woman?

²¹ For your ways are in full view of the LORD,
    and he examines all your paths.
²² The evil deeds of the wicked ensnare them;
    the cords of their sins hold them fast.
²³ For lack of discipline they will die,
    led astray by their own great folly.

## Warnings Against Folly

6 My son, if you have put up security for your neighbor,
    if you have shaken hands in pledge for a stranger,
² you have been trapped by what you said,
    ensnared by the words of your mouth.
³ So do this, my son, to free yourself,
    since you have fallen into your neighbor's hands:
    Go — to the point of exhaustion — ᵃ
    and give your neighbor no rest!
⁴ Allow no sleep to your eyes,
    no slumber to your eyelids.
⁵ Free yourself, like a gazelle from the hand of the hunter,
    like a bird from the snare of the fowler.

⁶ Go to the ant, you sluggard;
    consider its ways and be wise!
⁷ It has no commander,
    no overseer or ruler,
⁸ yet it stores its provisions in summer
    and gathers its food at harvest.

⁹ How long will you lie there, you sluggard?
    When will you get up from your sleep?
¹⁰ A little sleep, a little slumber,
    a little folding of the hands to rest —
¹¹ and poverty will come on you like a thief
    and scarcity like an armed man.

¹² A troublemaker and a villain,
    who goes about with a corrupt mouth,
¹³    who winks maliciously with his eye,
    signals with his feet
    and motions with his fingers,
¹⁴    who plots evil with deceit in his heart —
    he always stirs up conflict.
¹⁵ Therefore disaster will overtake him in an instant;
    he will suddenly be destroyed — without remedy.

¹⁶ There are six things the LORD hates,
    seven that are detestable to him:
¹⁷    haughty eyes,
    a lying tongue,
    hands that shed innocent blood,

ᵃ 3 Or *Go and humble yourself,*

18     a heart that devises wicked schemes,
       feet that are quick to rush into evil,
19     a false witness who pours out lies
       and a person who stirs up conflict in the
           community.

## Warning Against Adultery

20 My son, keep your father's command
     and do not forsake your mother's teaching.
21 Bind them always on your heart;
     fasten them around your neck.
22 When you walk, they will guide you;
     when you sleep, they will watch over you;
     when you awake, they will speak to you.
23 For this command is a lamp,
     this teaching is a light,
   and correction and instruction
     are the way to life,
24 keeping you from your neighbor's wife,
     from the smooth talk of a wayward woman.

25 Do not lust in your heart after her beauty
     or let her captivate you with her eyes.

26 For a prostitute can be had for a loaf of bread,
     but another man's wife preys on your very life.
27 Can a man scoop fire into his lap
     without his clothes being burned?
28 Can a man walk on hot coals
     without his feet being scorched?
29 So is he who sleeps with another man's wife;
     no one who touches her will go unpunished.

30 People do not despise a thief if he steals
     to satisfy his hunger when he is starving.
31 Yet if he is caught, he must pay sevenfold,
     though it costs him all the wealth of his house.
32 But a man who commits adultery has no sense;
     whoever does so destroys himself.
33 Blows and disgrace are his lot,
     and his shame will never be wiped away.

34 For jealousy arouses a husband's fury,
     and he will show no mercy when he takes revenge.
35 He will not accept any compensation;
     he will refuse a bribe, however great it is.

## Warning Against the Adulterous Woman

7 My son, keep my words
     and store up my commands within you.
2 Keep my commands and you will live;
     guard my teachings as the apple of your eye.
3 Bind them on your fingers;
     write them on the tablet of your heart.
4 Say to wisdom, "You are my sister,"
     and to insight, "You are my relative."

⁵ They will keep you from the adulterous woman,
from the wayward woman with her seductive words.

⁶ At the window of my house
I looked down through the lattice.
⁷ I saw among the simple,
I noticed among the young men,
a youth who had no sense.
⁸ He was going down the street near her corner,
walking along in the direction of her house
⁹ at twilight, as the day was fading,
as the dark of night set in.

¹⁰ Then out came a woman to meet him,
dressed like a prostitute and with crafty intent.
¹¹ (She is unruly and defiant,
her feet never stay at home;
¹² now in the street, now in the squares,
at every corner she lurks.)
¹³ She took hold of him and kissed him
and with a brazen face she said:

¹⁴ "Today I fulfilled my vows,
and I have food from my fellowship offering at home.
¹⁵ So I came out to meet you;
I looked for you and have found you!
¹⁶ I have covered my bed
with colored linens from Egypt.
¹⁷ I have perfumed my bed
with myrrh, aloes and cinnamon.
¹⁸ Come, let's drink deeply of love till morning;
let's enjoy ourselves with love!
¹⁹ My husband is not at home;
he has gone on a long journey.
²⁰ He took his purse filled with money
and will not be home till full moon."

²¹ With persuasive words she led him astray;
she seduced him with her smooth talk.
²² All at once he followed her
like an ox going to the slaughter,
like a deer[a] stepping into a noose[b]
²³     till an arrow pierces his liver,
like a bird darting into a snare,
little knowing it will cost him his life.

²⁴ Now then, my sons, listen to me;
pay attention to what I say.
²⁵ Do not let your heart turn to her ways
or stray into her paths.
²⁶ Many are the victims she has brought down;
her slain are a mighty throng.
²⁷ Her house is a highway to the grave,
leading down to the chambers of death.

---

[a] 22 Syriac (see also Septuagint); Hebrew *fool*     [b] 22 The meaning of the Hebrew for
this line is uncertain.

## Wisdom's Call

**8** Does not wisdom call out?
Does not understanding raise her voice?
² At the highest point along the way,
where the paths meet, she takes her stand;
³ beside the gate leading into the city,
at the entrance, she cries aloud:
⁴ "To you, O people, I call out;
I raise my voice to all mankind.
⁵ You who are simple, gain prudence;
you who are foolish, set your hearts on it.*ᵃ*
⁶ Listen, for I have trustworthy things to say;
I open my lips to speak what is right.
⁷ My mouth speaks what is true,
for my lips detest wickedness.
⁸ All the words of my mouth are just;
none of them is crooked or perverse.
⁹ To the discerning all of them are right;
they are upright to those who have found
knowledge.
¹⁰ Choose my instruction instead of silver,
knowledge rather than choice gold,
¹¹ for wisdom is more precious than rubies,
and nothing you desire can compare with her.

¹² "I, wisdom, dwell together with prudence;
I possess knowledge and discretion.
¹³ To fear the LORD is to hate evil;
I hate pride and arrogance,
evil behavior and perverse speech.
¹⁴ Counsel and sound judgment are mine;
I have insight, I have power.
¹⁵ By me kings reign
and rulers issue decrees that are just;
¹⁶ by me princes govern,
and nobles — all who rule on earth.*ᵇ*
¹⁷ I love those who love me,
and those who seek me find me.
¹⁸ With me are riches and honor,
enduring wealth and prosperity.
¹⁹ My fruit is better than fine gold;
what I yield surpasses choice silver.
²⁰ I walk in the way of righteousness,
along the paths of justice,
²¹ bestowing a rich inheritance on those who love me
and making their treasuries full.

²² "The LORD brought me forth as the first of his works,*ᶜ,ᵈ*
before his deeds of old;
²³ I was formed long ages ago,
at the very beginning, when the world came to be.

---

*ᵃ*5 Septuagint; Hebrew *foolish, instruct your minds*     *ᵇ*16 Some Hebrew manuscripts
and Septuagint; other Hebrew manuscripts *all righteous rulers*     *ᶜ*22 Or *way;* or
*dominion*     *ᵈ*22 Or *The LORD possessed me at the beginning of his work;* or *The LORD
brought me forth at the beginning of his work*

I walk in the way of righteousness, along the paths of justice.

PROVERBS 8:20

²⁴ When there were no watery depths, I was given birth,
 when there were no springs overflowing with water;
²⁵ before the mountains were settled in place,
 before the hills, I was given birth,
²⁶ before he made the world or its fields
 or any of the dust of the earth.
²⁷ I was there when he set the heavens in place,
 when he marked out the horizon on the face of the deep,
²⁸ when he established the clouds above
 and fixed securely the fountains of the deep,
²⁹ when he gave the sea its boundary
 so the waters would not overstep his command,
 and when he marked out the foundations of the earth.
³⁰  Then I was constantly*ᵃ* at his side.
 I was filled with delight day after day,
 rejoicing always in his presence,
³¹ rejoicing in his whole world
 and delighting in mankind.

³² "Now then, my children, listen to me;
 blessed are those who keep my ways.
³³ Listen to my instruction and be wise;
 do not disregard it.
³⁴ Blessed are those who listen to me,
 watching daily at my doors,
 waiting at my doorway.
³⁵ For those who find me find life
 and receive favor from the Lᴏʀᴅ.
³⁶ But those who fail to find me harm themselves;
 all who hate me love death."

## Invitations of Wisdom and Folly

9 Wisdom has built her house;
 she has set up*ᵇ* its seven pillars.
² She has prepared her meat and mixed her wine;
 she has also set her table.
³ She has sent out her servants, and she calls
 from the highest point of the city,
⁴  "Let all who are simple come to my house!"
 To those who have no sense she says,
⁵  "Come, eat my food
 and drink the wine I have mixed.
⁶ Leave your simple ways and you will live;
 walk in the way of insight."

⁷ Whoever corrects a mocker invites insults;
 whoever rebukes the wicked incurs abuse.
⁸ Do not rebuke mockers or they will hate you;
 rebuke the wise and they will love you.
⁹ Instruct the wise and they will be wiser still;
 teach the righteous and they will add to their learning.

¹⁰ The fear of the Lᴏʀᴅ is the beginning of wisdom,
 and knowledge of the Holy One is understanding.

---

ᵃ 30 Or *was the artisan*; or *was a little child*   ᵇ 1 Septuagint, Syriac and Targum;
Hebrew *has hewn out*

the
*fear*
of the LORD
is the
beginning of
**wisdom,**
and
knowledge
of the
*Holy One*
is
understanding.

*Proverbs
9:10*

¹¹ For through wisdom*a* your days will be many,
   and years will be added to your life.
¹² If you are wise, your wisdom will reward you;
   if you are a mocker, you alone will suffer.

¹³ Folly is an unruly woman;
   she is simple and knows nothing.
¹⁴ She sits at the door of her house,
   on a seat at the highest point of the city,
¹⁵ calling out to those who pass by,
   who go straight on their way,
¹⁶   "Let all who are simple come to my house!"
   To those who have no sense she says,
¹⁷   "Stolen water is sweet;
   food eaten in secret is delicious!"
¹⁸ But little do they know that the dead are there,
   that her guests are deep in the realm of the dead.

## Proverbs of Solomon

# 10
The proverbs of Solomon:

A wise son brings joy to his father,
   but a foolish son brings grief to his mother.

² Ill-gotten treasures have no lasting value,
   but righteousness delivers from death.

³ The LORD does not let the righteous go hungry,
   but he thwarts the craving of the wicked.

⁴ Lazy hands make for poverty,
   but diligent hands bring wealth.

⁵ He who gathers crops in summer is a prudent son,
   but he who sleeps during harvest is a disgraceful son.

⁶ Blessings crown the head of the righteous,
   but violence overwhelms the mouth of the wicked.*b*

⁷ The name of the righteous is used in blessings,*c*
   but the name of the wicked will rot.

⁸ The wise in heart accept commands,
   but a chattering fool comes to ruin.

⁹ Whoever walks in integrity walks securely,
   but whoever takes crooked paths will be found out.

¹⁰ Whoever winks maliciously causes grief,
   and a chattering fool comes to ruin.

¹¹ The mouth of the righteous is a fountain of life,
   but the mouth of the wicked conceals violence.

¹² Hatred stirs up conflict,
   but love covers over all wrongs.

¹³ Wisdom is found on the lips of the discerning,
   but a rod is for the back of one who has no sense.

---

*a* 11 Septuagint, Syriac and Targum; Hebrew *me*    *b* 6 Or *righteous, / but the mouth of the wicked conceals violence*    *c* 7 See Gen. 48:20.

Whoever walks in INTEGRITY walks securely.

Proverbs 10:9

[14] The wise store up knowledge,
　　but the mouth of a fool invites ruin.

[15] The wealth of the rich is their fortified city,
　　but poverty is the ruin of the poor.

[16] The wages of the righteous is life,
　　but the earnings of the wicked are sin and death.

[17] Whoever heeds discipline shows the way to life,
　　but whoever ignores correction leads others astray.

[18] Whoever conceals hatred with lying lips
　　and spreads slander is a fool.

[19] Sin is not ended by multiplying words,
　　but the prudent hold their tongues.

[20] The tongue of the righteous is choice silver,
　　but the heart of the wicked is of little value.

[21] The lips of the righteous nourish many,
　　but fools die for lack of sense.

[22] The blessing of the LORD brings wealth,
　　without painful toil for it.

[23] A fool finds pleasure in wicked schemes,
　　but a person of understanding delights in wisdom.

[24] What the wicked dread will overtake them;
　　what the righteous desire will be granted.

[25] When the storm has swept by, the wicked are gone,
　　but the righteous stand firm forever.

[26] As vinegar to the teeth and smoke to the eyes,
　　so are sluggards to those who send them.

[27] The fear of the LORD adds length to life,
　　but the years of the wicked are cut short.

[28] The prospect of the righteous is joy,
　　but the hopes of the wicked come to nothing.

[29] The way of the LORD is a refuge for the blameless,
　　but it is the ruin of those who do evil.

[30] The righteous will never be uprooted,
　　but the wicked will not remain in the land.

[31] From the mouth of the righteous comes the fruit of wisdom,
　　but a perverse tongue will be silenced.

[32] The lips of the righteous know what finds favor,
　　but the mouth of the wicked only what is perverse.

**11** The LORD detests dishonest scales,
　　but accurate weights find favor with him.

[2] When pride comes, then comes disgrace,
　　but with humility comes wisdom.

[3] The integrity of the upright guides them,
　　but the unfaithful are destroyed by their duplicity.

4 Wealth is worthless in the day of wrath,
   but righteousness delivers from death.

5 The righteousness of the blameless makes their paths straight,
   but the wicked are brought down by their own wickedness.

6 The righteousness of the upright delivers them,
   but the unfaithful are trapped by evil desires.

7 Hopes placed in mortals die with them;
   all the promise of[a] their power comes to nothing.

8 The righteous person is rescued from trouble,
   and it falls on the wicked instead.

9 With their mouths the godless destroy their neighbors,
   but through knowledge the righteous escape.

10 When the righteous prosper, the city rejoices;
   when the wicked perish, there are shouts of joy.

11 Through the blessing of the upright a city is exalted,
   but by the mouth of the wicked it is destroyed.

12 Whoever derides their neighbor has no sense,
   but the one who has understanding holds their tongue.

13 A gossip betrays a confidence,
   but a trustworthy person keeps a secret.

14 For lack of guidance a nation falls,
   but victory is won through many advisers.

15 Whoever puts up security for a stranger will surely suffer,
   but whoever refuses to shake hands in pledge is safe.

16 A kindhearted woman gains honor,
   but ruthless men gain only wealth.

17 Those who are kind benefit themselves,
   but the cruel bring ruin on themselves.

18 A wicked person earns deceptive wages,
   but the one who sows righteousness reaps a sure reward.

19 Truly the righteous attain life,
   but whoever pursues evil finds death.

20 The LORD detests those whose hearts are perverse,
   but he delights in those whose ways are blameless.

21 Be sure of this: The wicked will not go unpunished,
   but those who are righteous will go free.

22 Like a gold ring in a pig's snout
   is a beautiful woman who shows no discretion.

23 The desire of the righteous ends only in good,
   but the hope of the wicked only in wrath.

24 One person gives freely, yet gains even more;
   another withholds unduly, but comes to poverty.

---

[a] 7 Two Hebrew manuscripts; most Hebrew manuscripts, Vulgate, Syriac and Targum
*When the wicked die, their hope perishes; / all they expected from*

A kind-hearted woman gains honor

Proverbs 11:16

²⁵ A generous person will prosper;
   whoever refreshes others will be refreshed.

²⁶ People curse the one who hoards grain,
   but they pray God's blessing on the one who is willing to sell.

²⁷ Whoever seeks good finds favor,
   but evil comes to one who searches for it.

²⁸ Those who trust in their riches will fall,
   but the righteous will thrive like a green leaf.

²⁹ Whoever brings ruin on their family will inherit only wind,
   and the fool will be servant to the wise.

³⁰ The fruit of the righteous is a tree of life,
   and the one who is wise saves lives.

³¹ If the righteous receive their due on earth,
   how much more the ungodly and the sinner!

**12** Whoever loves discipline loves knowledge,
   but whoever hates correction is stupid.

² Good people obtain favor from the LORD,
   but he condemns those who devise wicked schemes.

³ No one can be established through wickedness,
   but the righteous cannot be uprooted.

⁴ A wife of noble character is her husband's crown,
   but a disgraceful wife is like decay in his bones.

⁵ The plans of the righteous are just,
   but the advice of the wicked is deceitful.

⁶ The words of the wicked lie in wait for blood,
   but the speech of the upright rescues them.

⁷ The wicked are overthrown and are no more,
   but the house of the righteous stands firm.

⁸ A person is praised according to their prudence,
   and one with a warped mind is despised.

⁹ Better to be a nobody and yet have a servant
   than pretend to be somebody and have no food.

¹⁰ The righteous care for the needs of their animals,
   but the kindest acts of the wicked are cruel.

¹¹ Those who work their land will have abundant food,
   but those who chase fantasies have no sense.

¹² The wicked desire the stronghold of evildoers,
   but the root of the righteous endures.

¹³ Evildoers are trapped by their sinful talk,
   and so the innocent escape trouble.

¹⁴ From the fruit of their lips people are filled with good things,
   and the work of their hands brings them reward.

¹⁵ The way of fools seems right to them,
   but the wise listen to advice.

¹⁶ Fools show their annoyance at once,
  but the prudent overlook an insult.

¹⁷ An honest witness tells the truth,
  but a false witness tells lies.

¹⁸ The words of the reckless pierce like swords,
  but the tongue of the wise brings healing.

¹⁹ Truthful lips endure forever,
  but a lying tongue lasts only a moment.

²⁰ Deceit is in the hearts of those who plot evil,
  but those who promote peace have joy.

²¹ No harm overtakes the righteous,
  but the wicked have their fill of trouble.

²² The LORD detests lying lips,
  but he delights in people who are trustworthy.

²³ The prudent keep their knowledge to themselves,
  but a fool's heart blurts out folly.

²⁴ Diligent hands will rule,
  but laziness ends in forced labor.

²⁵ Anxiety weighs down the heart,
  but a kind word cheers it up.

²⁶ The righteous choose their friends carefully,
  but the way of the wicked leads them astray.

²⁷ The lazy do not roast*ᵃ* any game,
  but the diligent feed on the riches of the hunt.

²⁸ In the way of righteousness there is life;
  along that path is immortality.

**13** A wise son heeds his father's instruction,
  but a mocker does not respond to rebukes.

² From the fruit of their lips people enjoy good things,
  but the unfaithful have an appetite for violence.

³ Those who guard their lips preserve their lives,
  but those who speak rashly will come to ruin.

⁴ A sluggard's appetite is never filled,
  but the desires of the diligent are fully satisfied.

⁵ The righteous hate what is false,
  but the wicked make themselves a stench
  and bring shame on themselves.

⁶ Righteousness guards the person of integrity,
  but wickedness overthrows the sinner.

⁷ One person pretends to be rich, yet has nothing;
  another pretends to be poor, yet has great wealth.

⁸ A person's riches may ransom their life,
  but the poor cannot respond to threatening rebukes.

---

*ᵃ 27* The meaning of the Hebrew for this word is uncertain.

proverbs 12:25

Anxiety weighs down the heart, but a kind word cheers it up.

⁹ The light of the righteous shines brightly,
  but the lamp of the wicked is snuffed out.

¹⁰ Where there is strife, there is pride,
  but wisdom is found in those who take advice.

¹¹ Dishonest money dwindles away,
  but whoever gathers money little by little makes
    it grow.

¹² Hope deferred makes the heart sick,
  but a longing fulfilled is a tree of life.

¹³ Whoever scorns instruction will pay for it,
  but whoever respects a command is rewarded.

¹⁴ The teaching of the wise is a fountain of life,
  turning a person from the snares of death.

¹⁵ Good judgment wins favor,
  but the way of the unfaithful leads to their destruction.ᵃ

¹⁶ All who are prudent act withᵇ knowledge,
  but fools expose their folly.

¹⁷ A wicked messenger falls into trouble,
  but a trustworthy envoy brings healing.

¹⁸ Whoever disregards discipline comes to poverty and shame,
  but whoever heeds correction is honored.

¹⁹ A longing fulfilled is sweet to the soul,
  but fools detest turning from evil.

²⁰ Walk with the wise and become wise,
  for a companion of fools suffers harm.

²¹ Trouble pursues the sinner,
  but the righteous are rewarded with good things.

²² A good person leaves an inheritance for their children's
    children,
  but a sinner's wealth is stored up for the righteous.

²³ An unplowed field produces food for the poor,
  but injustice sweeps it away.

²⁴ Whoever spares the rod hates their children,
  but the one who loves their children is careful to
    discipline them.

²⁵ The righteous eat to their hearts' content,
  but the stomach of the wicked goes hungry.

14 The wise woman builds her house,
  but with her own hands the foolish one tears hers down.

² Whoever fears the LORD walks uprightly,
  but those who despise him are devious in their ways.

³ A fool's mouth lashes out with pride,
  but the lips of the wise protect them.

---

ᵃ 15 Septuagint and Syriac; the meaning of the Hebrew for this phrase is uncertain.
ᵇ 16 Or *prudent protect themselves through*

⁴ Where there are no oxen, the manger is empty,
　but from the strength of an ox come abundant harvests.

⁵ An honest witness does not deceive,
　but a false witness pours out lies.

⁶ The mocker seeks wisdom and finds none,
　but knowledge comes easily to the discerning.

⁷ Stay away from a fool,
　for you will not find knowledge on their lips.

⁸ The wisdom of the prudent is to give thought to their ways,
　but the folly of fools is deception.

⁹ Fools mock at making amends for sin,
　but goodwill is found among the upright.

¹⁰ Each heart knows its own bitterness,
　and no one else can share its joy.

¹¹ The house of the wicked will be destroyed,
　but the tent of the upright will flourish.

¹² There is a way that appears to be right,
　but in the end it leads to death.

¹³ Even in laughter the heart may ache,
　and rejoicing may end in grief.

¹⁴ The faithless will be fully repaid for their ways,
　and the good rewarded for theirs.

¹⁵ The simple believe anything,
　but the prudent give thought to their steps.

¹⁶ The wise fear the LORD and shun evil,
　but a fool is hotheaded and yet feels secure.

¹⁷ A quick-tempered person does foolish things,
　and the one who devises evil schemes is hated.

¹⁸ The simple inherit folly,
　but the prudent are crowned with knowledge.

¹⁹ Evildoers will bow down in the presence of the good,
　and the wicked at the gates of the righteous.

²⁰ The poor are shunned even by their neighbors,
　but the rich have many friends.

²¹ It is a sin to despise one's neighbor,
　but blessed is the one who is kind to the needy.

²² Do not those who plot evil go astray?
　But those who plan what is good find*a* love and
　faithfulness.

²³ All hard work brings a profit,
　but mere talk leads only to poverty.

²⁴ The wealth of the wise is their crown,
　but the folly of fools yields folly.

*a 22* Or *show*

²⁵ A truthful witness saves lives,
  but a false witness is deceitful.

²⁶ Whoever fears the LORD has a secure fortress,
  and for their children it will be a refuge.

²⁷ The fear of the LORD is a fountain of life,
  turning a person from the snares of death.

²⁸ A large population is a king's glory,
  but without subjects a prince is ruined.

²⁹ Whoever is patient has great understanding,
  but one who is quick-tempered displays folly.

³⁰ A heart at peace gives life to the body,
  but envy rots the bones.

³¹ Whoever oppresses the poor shows contempt for their Maker,
  but whoever is kind to the needy honors God.

³² When calamity comes, the wicked are brought down,
  but even in death the righteous seek refuge in God.

³³ Wisdom reposes in the heart of the discerning
  and even among fools she lets herself be known.[a]

³⁴ Righteousness exalts a nation,
  but sin condemns any people.

³⁵ A king delights in a wise servant,
  but a shameful servant arouses his fury.

**15** A gentle answer turns away wrath,
  but a harsh word stirs up anger.

² The tongue of the wise adorns knowledge,
  but the mouth of the fool gushes folly.

³ The eyes of the LORD are everywhere,
  keeping watch on the wicked and the good.

⁴ The soothing tongue is a tree of life,
  but a perverse tongue crushes the spirit.

⁵ A fool spurns a parent's discipline,
  but whoever heeds correction shows prudence.

⁶ The house of the righteous contains great treasure,
  but the income of the wicked brings ruin.

⁷ The lips of the wise spread knowledge,
  but the hearts of fools are not upright.

⁸ The LORD detests the sacrifice of the wicked,
  but the prayer of the upright pleases him.

⁹ The LORD detests the way of the wicked,
  but he loves those who pursue righteousness.

¹⁰ Stern discipline awaits anyone who leaves the path;
  the one who hates correction will die.

---

[a] 33 Hebrew; Septuagint and Syriac *discerning / but in the heart of fools she is not known*

A gentle ANSWER TURNS AWAY wrath, BUT A harsh word STIRS UP anger.

PROVERBS 15:1

<sup>11</sup> Death and Destruction<sup>a</sup> lie open before the LORD —
  how much more do human hearts!

<sup>12</sup> Mockers resent correction,
  so they avoid the wise.

<sup>13</sup> A happy heart makes the face cheerful,
  but heartache crushes the spirit.

<sup>14</sup> The discerning heart seeks knowledge,
  but the mouth of a fool feeds on folly.

<sup>15</sup> All the days of the oppressed are wretched,
  but the cheerful heart has a continual feast.

<sup>16</sup> Better a little with the fear of the LORD
  than great wealth with turmoil.

<sup>17</sup> Better a small serving of vegetables with love
  than a fattened calf with hatred.

<sup>18</sup> A hot-tempered person stirs up conflict,
  but the one who is patient calms a quarrel.

<sup>19</sup> The way of the sluggard is blocked with thorns,
  but the path of the upright is a highway.

<sup>20</sup> A wise son brings joy to his father,
  but a foolish man despises his mother.

<sup>21</sup> Folly brings joy to one who has no sense,
  but whoever has understanding keeps a straight
    course.

<sup>22</sup> Plans fail for lack of counsel,
  but with many advisers they succeed.

<sup>23</sup> A person finds joy in giving an apt reply —
  and how good is a timely word!

<sup>24</sup> The path of life leads upward for the prudent
  to keep them from going down to the realm of
    the dead.

<sup>25</sup> The LORD tears down the house of the proud,
  but he sets the widow's boundary stones in place.

<sup>26</sup> The LORD detests the thoughts of the wicked,
  but gracious words are pure in his sight.

<sup>27</sup> The greedy bring ruin to their households,
  but the one who hates bribes will live.

<sup>28</sup> The heart of the righteous weighs its answers,
  but the mouth of the wicked gushes evil.

<sup>29</sup> The LORD is far from the wicked,
  but he hears the prayer of the righteous.

<sup>30</sup> Light in a messenger's eyes brings joy to the
    heart,
  and good news gives health to the bones.

---

<sup>a</sup> 11 Hebrew *Abaddon*

31 Whoever heeds life-giving correction
   will be at home among the wise.

32 Those who disregard discipline despise themselves,
   but the one who heeds correction gains understanding.

33 Wisdom's instruction is to fear the LORD,
   and humility comes before honor.

**16** To humans belong the plans of the heart,
   but from the LORD comes the proper answer of the tongue.

2 All a person's ways seem pure to them,
   but motives are weighed by the LORD.

3 Commit to the LORD whatever you do,
   and he will establish your plans.

4 The LORD works out everything to its proper end —
   even the wicked for a day of disaster.

5 The LORD detests all the proud of heart.
   Be sure of this: They will not go unpunished.

6 Through love and faithfulness sin is atoned for;
   through the fear of the LORD evil is avoided.

7 When the LORD takes pleasure in anyone's way,
   he causes their enemies to make peace with them.

8 Better a little with righteousness
   than much gain with injustice.

9 In their hearts humans plan their course,
   but the LORD establishes their steps.

10 The lips of a king speak as an oracle,
   and his mouth does not betray justice.

11 Honest scales and balances belong to the LORD;
   all the weights in the bag are of his making.

12 Kings detest wrongdoing,
   for a throne is established through righteousness.

13 Kings take pleasure in honest lips;
   they value the one who speaks what is right.

14 A king's wrath is a messenger of death,
   but the wise will appease it.

15 When a king's face brightens, it means life;
   his favor is like a rain cloud in spring.

16 How much better to get wisdom than gold,
   to get insight rather than silver!

17 The highway of the upright avoids evil;
   those who guard their ways preserve their lives.

18 Pride goes before destruction,
   a haughty spirit before a fall.

19 Better to be lowly in spirit along with the oppressed
   than to share plunder with the proud.

COMMIT TO THE LORD WHATEVER YOU DO & HE WILL ESTABLISH YOUR PLANS.

**PROVERBS 16:3**

20 Whoever gives heed to instruction prospers,<sup>a</sup>
    and blessed is the one who trusts in the LORD.

21 The wise in heart are called discerning,
    and gracious words promote instruction.<sup>b</sup>

22 Prudence is a fountain of life to the prudent,
    but folly brings punishment to fools.

23 The hearts of the wise make their mouths prudent,
    and their lips promote instruction.<sup>c</sup>

24 Gracious words are a honeycomb,
    sweet to the soul and healing to the bones.

25 There is a way that appears to be right,
    but in the end it leads to death.

26 The appetite of laborers works for them;
    their hunger drives them on.

27 A scoundrel plots evil,
    and on their lips it is like a scorching fire.

28 A perverse person stirs up conflict,
    and a gossip separates close friends.

29 A violent person entices their neighbor
    and leads them down a path that is not good.

30 Whoever winks with their eye is plotting perversity;
    whoever purses their lips is bent on evil.

31 Gray hair is a crown of splendor;
    it is attained in the way of righteousness.

32 Better a patient person than a warrior,
    one with self-control than one who takes a city.

33 The lot is cast into the lap,
    but its every decision is from the LORD.

**17** Better a dry crust with peace and quiet
    than a house full of feasting, with strife.

2 A prudent servant will rule over a disgraceful son
    and will share the inheritance as one of the family.

3 The crucible for silver and the furnace for gold,
    but the LORD tests the heart.

4 A wicked person listens to deceitful lips;
    a liar pays attention to a destructive tongue.

5 Whoever mocks the poor shows contempt for their Maker;
    whoever gloats over disaster will not go unpunished.

6 Children's children are a crown to the aged,
    and parents are the pride of their children.

7 Eloquent lips are unsuited to a godless fool —
    how much worse lying lips to a ruler!

---

<sup>a</sup> 20 Or *whoever speaks prudently finds what is good*    <sup>b</sup> 21 Or *words make a person persuasive*    <sup>c</sup> 23 Or *prudent / and make their lips persuasive*

⁸ A bribe is seen as a charm by the one who gives it;
   they think success will come at every turn.

⁹ Whoever would foster love covers over an offense,
   but whoever repeats the matter separates close friends.

¹⁰ A rebuke impresses a discerning person
   more than a hundred lashes a fool.

¹¹ Evildoers foster rebellion against God;
   the messenger of death will be sent against them.

¹² Better to meet a bear robbed of her cubs
   than a fool bent on folly.

¹³ Evil will never leave the house
   of one who pays back evil for good.

¹⁴ Starting a quarrel is like breaching a dam;
   so drop the matter before a dispute breaks out.

¹⁵ Acquitting the guilty and condemning the innocent —
   the Lᴏʀᴅ detests them both.

¹⁶ Why should fools have money in hand to buy wisdom,
   when they are not able to understand it?

¹⁷ A friend loves at all times,
   and a brother is born for a time of adversity.

¹⁸ One who has no sense shakes hands in pledge
   and puts up security for a neighbor.

¹⁹ Whoever loves a quarrel loves sin;
   whoever builds a high gate invites destruction.

²⁰ One whose heart is corrupt does not prosper;
   one whose tongue is perverse falls into trouble.

²¹ To have a fool for a child brings grief;
   there is no joy for the parent of a godless fool.

²² A cheerful heart is good medicine,
   but a crushed spirit dries up the bones.

²³ The wicked accept bribes in secret
   to pervert the course of justice.

²⁴ A discerning person keeps wisdom in view,
   but a fool's eyes wander to the ends of the earth.

²⁵ A foolish son brings grief to his father
   and bitterness to the mother who bore him.

²⁶ If imposing a fine on the innocent is not good,
   surely to flog honest officials is not right.

²⁷ The one who has knowledge uses words with restraint,
   and whoever has understanding is even-tempered.

²⁸ Even fools are thought wise if they keep silent,
   and discerning if they hold their tongues.

**18** An unfriendly person pursues selfish ends
   and against all sound judgment starts quarrels.

2 Fools find no pleasure in understanding
  but delight in airing their own opinions.

3 When wickedness comes, so does contempt,
  and with shame comes reproach.

4 The words of the mouth are deep waters,
  but the fountain of wisdom is a rushing stream.

5 It is not good to be partial to the wicked
  and so deprive the innocent of justice.

6 The lips of fools bring them strife,
  and their mouths invite a beating.

7 The mouths of fools are their undoing,
  and their lips are a snare to their very lives.

8 The words of a gossip are like choice morsels;
  they go down to the inmost parts.

9 One who is slack in his work
  is brother to one who destroys.

10 The name of the LORD is a fortified tower;
  the righteous run to it and are safe.

11 The wealth of the rich is their fortified city;
  they imagine it a wall too high to scale.

12 Before a downfall the heart is haughty,
  but humility comes before honor.

13 To answer before listening —
  that is folly and shame.

14 The human spirit can endure in sickness,
  but a crushed spirit who can bear?

15 The heart of the discerning acquires knowledge,
  for the ears of the wise seek it out.

16 A gift opens the way
  and ushers the giver into the presence of the great.

17 In a lawsuit the first to speak seems right,
  until someone comes forward and cross-examines.

18 Casting the lot settles disputes
  and keeps strong opponents apart.

19 A brother wronged is more unyielding than a fortified city;
  disputes are like the barred gates of a citadel.

20 From the fruit of their mouth a person's stomach is filled;
  with the harvest of their lips they are satisfied.

21 The tongue has the power of life and death,
  and those who love it will eat its fruit.

22 He who finds a wife finds what is good
  and receives favor from the LORD.

23 The poor plead for mercy,
  but the rich answer harshly.

²⁴One who has unreliable friends soon comes to ruin,
but there is a friend who sticks closer than a brother.

**19** Better the poor whose walk is blameless
than a fool whose lips are perverse.

²Desire without knowledge is not good —
how much more will hasty feet miss the way!

³A person's own folly leads to their ruin,
yet their heart rages against the Lord.

⁴Wealth attracts many friends,
but even the closest friend of the poor person deserts them.

⁵A false witness will not go unpunished,
and whoever pours out lies will not go free.

⁶Many curry favor with a ruler,
and everyone is the friend of one who gives gifts.

⁷The poor are shunned by all their relatives —
how much more do their friends avoid them!
Though the poor pursue them with pleading,
they are nowhere to be found.ᵃ

⁸The one who gets wisdom loves life;
the one who cherishes understanding will soon prosper.

⁹A false witness will not go unpunished,
and whoever pours out lies will perish.

¹⁰It is not fitting for a fool to live in luxury —
how much worse for a slave to rule over princes!

¹¹A person's wisdom yields patience;
it is to one's glory to overlook an offense.

¹²A king's rage is like the roar of a lion,
but his favor is like dew on the grass.

¹³A foolish child is a father's ruin,
and a quarrelsome wife is like
the constant dripping of a leaky roof.

¹⁴Houses and wealth are inherited from parents,
but a prudent wife is from the Lord.

¹⁵Laziness brings on deep sleep,
and the shiftless go hungry.

¹⁶Whoever keeps commandments keeps their life,
but whoever shows contempt for their ways will die.

¹⁷Whoever is kind to the poor lends to the Lord,
and he will reward them for what they have done.

¹⁸Discipline your children, for in that there is hope;
do not be a willing party to their death.

¹⁹A hot-tempered person must pay the penalty;
rescue them, and you will have to do it again.

ᵃ7 The meaning of the Hebrew for this sentence is uncertain.

one who has unreliable friends soon comes to ruin, but there is a friend who sticks closer than a brother.

PROVERBS 18:24

20 Listen to advice and accept discipline,
   and at the end you will be counted among the wise.

21 Many are the plans in a person's heart,
   but it is the LORD's purpose that prevails.

22 What a person desires is unfailing love*a*;
   better to be poor than a liar.

23 The fear of the LORD leads to life;
   then one rests content, untouched by trouble.

24 A sluggard buries his hand in the dish;
   he will not even bring it back to his mouth!

25 Flog a mocker, and the simple will learn prudence;
   rebuke the discerning, and they will gain
      knowledge.

26 Whoever robs their father and drives out their mother
   is a child who brings shame and disgrace.

27 Stop listening to instruction, my son,
   and you will stray from the words of knowledge.

28 A corrupt witness mocks at justice,
   and the mouth of the wicked gulps down evil.

29 Penalties are prepared for mockers,
   and beatings for the backs of fools.

**20** Wine is a mocker and beer a brawler;
   whoever is led astray by them is not wise.

2 A king's wrath strikes terror like the roar of a lion;
   those who anger him forfeit their lives.

3 It is to one's honor to avoid strife,
   but every fool is quick to quarrel.

4 Sluggards do not plow in season;
   so at harvest time they look but find nothing.

5 The purposes of a person's heart are deep waters,
   but one who has insight draws them out.

6 Many claim to have unfailing love,
   but a faithful person who can find?

7 The righteous lead blameless lives;
   blessed are their children after them.

8 When a king sits on his throne to judge,
   he winnows out all evil with his eyes.

9 Who can say, "I have kept my heart pure;
   I am clean and without sin"?

10 Differing weights and differing measures —
   the LORD detests them both.

11 Even small children are known by their actions,
   so is their conduct really pure and upright?

---

*a 22* Or *Greed is a person's shame*

MANY are the PLANS in a PERSON'S heart, BUT IT is the LORD'S purpose THAT prevails.

PROVERBS 19:21

¹² Ears that hear and eyes that see —
  the Lord has made them both.

¹³ Do not love sleep or you will grow poor;
  stay awake and you will have food to spare.

¹⁴ "It's no good, it's no good!" says the buyer —
  then goes off and boasts about the purchase.

¹⁵ Gold there is, and rubies in abundance,
  but lips that speak knowledge are a rare jewel.

¹⁶ Take the garment of one who puts up security for a
    stranger;
  hold it in pledge if it is done for an outsider.

¹⁷ Food gained by fraud tastes sweet,
  but one ends up with a mouth full of gravel.

¹⁸ Plans are established by seeking advice;
  so if you wage war, obtain guidance.

¹⁹ A gossip betrays a confidence;
  so avoid anyone who talks too much.

²⁰ If someone curses their father or mother,
  their lamp will be snuffed out in pitch darkness.

²¹ An inheritance claimed too soon
  will not be blessed at the end.

²² Do not say, "I'll pay you back for this wrong!"
  Wait for the Lord, and he will avenge you.

²³ The Lord detests differing weights,
  and dishonest scales do not please him.

²⁴ A person's steps are directed by the Lord.
  How then can anyone understand their own way?

²⁵ It is a trap to dedicate something rashly
  and only later to consider one's vows.

²⁶ A wise king winnows out the wicked;
  he drives the threshing wheel over them.

²⁷ The human spirit is*a* the lamp of the Lord
  that sheds light on one's inmost being.

²⁸ Love and faithfulness keep a king safe;
  through love his throne is made secure.

²⁹ The glory of young men is their strength,
  gray hair the splendor of the old.

³⁰ Blows and wounds scrub away evil,
  and beatings purge the inmost being.

**21** In the Lord's hand the king's heart is a stream of water
  that he channels toward all who please him.

² A person may think their own ways are right,
  but the Lord weighs the heart.

---

*a 27* Or *A person's words are*

³ To do what is right and just
　　is more acceptable to the LORD than sacrifice.

⁴ Haughty eyes and a proud heart —
　　the unplowed field of the wicked — produce sin.

⁵ The plans of the diligent lead to profit
　　as surely as haste leads to poverty.

⁶ A fortune made by a lying tongue
　　is a fleeting vapor and a deadly snare.ᵃ

⁷ The violence of the wicked will drag them away,
　　for they refuse to do what is right.

⁸ The way of the guilty is devious,
　　but the conduct of the innocent is upright.

⁹ Better to live on a corner of the roof
　　than share a house with a quarrelsome wife.

¹⁰ The wicked crave evil;
　　their neighbors get no mercy from them.

¹¹ When a mocker is punished, the simple gain wisdom;
　　by paying attention to the wise they get knowledge.

¹² The Righteous Oneᵇ takes note of the house of the wicked
　　and brings the wicked to ruin.

¹³ Whoever shuts their ears to the cry of the poor
　　will also cry out and not be answered.

¹⁴ A gift given in secret soothes anger,
　　and a bribe concealed in the cloak pacifies great wrath.

¹⁵ When justice is done, it brings joy to the righteous
　　but terror to evildoers.

¹⁶ Whoever strays from the path of prudence
　　comes to rest in the company of the dead.

¹⁷ Whoever loves pleasure will become poor;
　　whoever loves wine and olive oil will never be rich.

¹⁸ The wicked become a ransom for the righteous,
　　and the unfaithful for the upright.

¹⁹ Better to live in a desert
　　than with a quarrelsome and nagging wife.

²⁰ The wise store up choice food and olive oil,
　　but fools gulp theirs down.

²¹ Whoever pursues righteousness and love
　　finds life, prosperityᶜ and honor.

²² One who is wise can go up against the city of the mighty
　　and pull down the stronghold in which they trust.

²³ Those who guard their mouths and their tongues
　　keep themselves from calamity.

ᵃ 6 Some Hebrew manuscripts, Septuagint and Vulgate; most Hebrew manuscripts
*vapor for those who seek death*　　ᵇ 12 Or *The righteous person*　　ᶜ 21 Or *righteousness*

WHEN *Justice* IS DONE, IT BRINGS *Joy* TO THE *Righteous.*

PROVERBS 21:15

<sup>24</sup> The proud and arrogant person — "Mocker" is his name —
  behaves with insolent fury.

<sup>25</sup> The craving of a sluggard will be the death of him,
  because his hands refuse to work.
<sup>26</sup> All day long he craves for more,
  but the righteous give without sparing.

<sup>27</sup> The sacrifice of the wicked is detestable —
  how much more so when brought with evil intent!

<sup>28</sup> A false witness will perish,
  but a careful listener will testify successfully.

<sup>29</sup> The wicked put up a bold front,
  but the upright give thought to their ways.

<sup>30</sup> There is no wisdom, no insight, no plan
  that can succeed against the LORD.

<sup>31</sup> The horse is made ready for the day of battle,
  but victory rests with the LORD.

**22** A good name is more desirable than great riches;
  to be esteemed is better than silver or gold.

<sup>2</sup> Rich and poor have this in common:
  The LORD is the Maker of them all.

<sup>3</sup> The prudent see danger and take refuge,
  but the simple keep going and pay the penalty.

<sup>4</sup> Humility is the fear of the LORD;
  its wages are riches and honor and life.

<sup>5</sup> In the paths of the wicked are snares and pitfalls,
  but those who would preserve their life stay far from them.

<sup>6</sup> Start children off on the way they should go,
  and even when they are old they will not turn from it.

<sup>7</sup> The rich rule over the poor,
  and the borrower is slave to the lender.

<sup>8</sup> Whoever sows injustice reaps calamity,
  and the rod they wield in fury will be broken.

<sup>9</sup> The generous will themselves be blessed,
  for they share their food with the poor.

<sup>10</sup> Drive out the mocker, and out goes strife;
  quarrels and insults are ended.

<sup>11</sup> One who loves a pure heart and who speaks with grace
  will have the king for a friend.

<sup>12</sup> The eyes of the LORD keep watch over knowledge,
  but he frustrates the words of the unfaithful.

<sup>13</sup> The sluggard says, "There's a lion outside!
  I'll be killed in the public square!"

<sup>14</sup> The mouth of an adulterous woman is a deep pit;
  a man who is under the LORD's wrath falls into it.

start children off on the way they should go, and even when they are old they will not turn from it.

*PROVERBS 22:6*

¹⁵ Folly is bound up in the heart of a child,
　　but the rod of discipline will drive it far away.

¹⁶ One who oppresses the poor to increase his wealth
　　and one who gives gifts to the rich — both come to poverty.

## Thirty Sayings of the Wise

Saying 1

¹⁷ Pay attention and turn your ear to the sayings of the wise;
　　apply your heart to what I teach,
¹⁸ for it is pleasing when you keep them in your heart
　　and have all of them ready on your lips.
¹⁹ So that your trust may be in the LORD,
　　I teach you today, even you.
²⁰ Have I not written thirty sayings for you,
　　sayings of counsel and knowledge,
²¹ teaching you to be honest and to speak the truth,
　　so that you bring back truthful reports
　　to those you serve?

*Saying 2*

²² Do not exploit the poor because they are poor
　　and do not crush the needy in court,
²³ for the LORD will take up their case
　　and will exact life for life.

*Saying 3*

²⁴ Do not make friends with a hot-tempered person,
　　do not associate with one easily angered,
²⁵ or you may learn their ways
　　and get yourself ensnared.

*Saying 4*

²⁶ Do not be one who shakes hands in pledge
　　or puts up security for debts;
²⁷ if you lack the means to pay,
　　your very bed will be snatched from under you.

*Saying 5*

²⁸ Do not move an ancient boundary stone
　　set up by your ancestors.

*Saying 6*

²⁹ Do you see someone skilled in their work?
　　They will serve before kings;
　　they will not serve before officials of low rank.

*Saying 7*

**23** When you sit to dine with a ruler,
　　note well what[a] is before you,
² and put a knife to your throat
　　if you are given to gluttony.
³ Do not crave his delicacies,
　　for that food is deceptive.

---

[a] 1 Or *who*

*Saying 8*

⁴ Do not wear yourself out to get rich;
  do not trust your own cleverness.
⁵ Cast but a glance at riches, and they are gone,
  for they will surely sprout wings
  and fly off to the sky like an eagle.

*Saying 9*

⁶ Do not eat the food of a begrudging host,
  do not crave his delicacies;
⁷ for he is the kind of person
  who is always thinking about the cost.ᵃ
  "Eat and drink," he says to you,
  but his heart is not with you.
⁸ You will vomit up the little you have eaten
  and will have wasted your compliments.

*Saying 10*

⁹ Do not speak to fools,
  for they will scorn your prudent words.

*Saying 11*

¹⁰ Do not move an ancient boundary stone
  or encroach on the fields of the fatherless,
¹¹ for their Defender is strong;
  he will take up their case against you.

*Saying 12*

¹² Apply your heart to instruction
  and your ears to words of knowledge.

*Saying 13*

¹³ Do not withhold discipline from a child;
  if you punish them with the rod, they will not die.
¹⁴ Punish them with the rod
  and save them from death.

*Saying 14*

¹⁵ My son, if your heart is wise,
  then my heart will be glad indeed;
¹⁶ my inmost being will rejoice
  when your lips speak what is right.

*Saying 15*

¹⁷ Do not let your heart envy sinners,
  but always be zealous for the fear of the LORD.
¹⁸ There is surely a future hope for you,
  and your hope will not be cut off.

*Saying 16*

¹⁹ Listen, my son, and be wise,
  and set your heart on the right path:
²⁰ Do not join those who drink too much wine
  or gorge themselves on meat,

---

ᵃ 7 Or *for as he thinks within himself, / so he is*; or *for as he puts on a feast, / so he is*

21 for drunkards and gluttons become poor,
and drowsiness clothes them in rags.

*Saying 17*

22 Listen to your father, who gave you life,
and do not despise your mother when she is old.
23 Buy the truth and do not sell it —
wisdom, instruction and insight as well.
24 The father of a righteous child has great joy;
a man who fathers a wise son rejoices in him.
25 May your father and mother rejoice;
may she who gave you birth be joyful!

*Saying 18*

26 My son, give me your heart
and let your eyes delight in my ways,
27 for an adulterous woman is a deep pit,
and a wayward wife is a narrow well.
28 Like a bandit she lies in wait
and multiplies the unfaithful among men.

*Saying 19*

29 Who has woe? Who has sorrow?
Who has strife? Who has complaints?
Who has needless bruises? Who has bloodshot eyes?
30 Those who linger over wine,
who go to sample bowls of mixed wine.
31 Do not gaze at wine when it is red,
when it sparkles in the cup,
when it goes down smoothly!
32 In the end it bites like a snake
and poisons like a viper.
33 Your eyes will see strange sights,
and your mind will imagine confusing things.
34 You will be like one sleeping on the high seas,
lying on top of the rigging.
35 "They hit me," you will say, "but I'm not hurt!
They beat me, but I don't feel it!
When will I wake up
so I can find another drink?"

*Saying 20*

24 Do not envy the wicked,
do not desire their company;
2 for their hearts plot violence,
and their lips talk about making trouble.

*Saying 21*

3 By wisdom a house is built,
and through understanding it is established;
4 through knowledge its rooms are filled
with rare and beautiful treasures.

*Saying 22*

5 The wise prevail through great power,
and those who have knowledge muster their strength.

BY WISDOM A HOUSE IS BUILT.

PROVERBS 24:3

6 Surely you need guidance to wage war,
    and victory is won through many advisers.

*Saying 23*

7 Wisdom is too high for fools;
    in the assembly at the gate they must not open
        their mouths.

*Saying 24*

8 Whoever plots evil
    will be known as a schemer.
9 The schemes of folly are sin,
    and people detest a mocker.

*Saying 25*

10 If you falter in a time of trouble,
    how small is your strength!
11 Rescue those being led away to death;
    hold back those staggering toward slaughter.
12 If you say, "But we knew nothing about this,"
    does not he who weighs the heart perceive it?
Does not he who guards your life know it?
    Will he not repay everyone according to what they
        have done?

*Saying 26*

13 Eat honey, my son, for it is good;
    honey from the comb is sweet to your taste.
14 Know also that wisdom is like honey for you:
    If you find it, there is a future hope for you,
    and your hope will not be cut off.

*Saying 27*

15 Do not lurk like a thief near the house of the righteous,
    do not plunder their dwelling place;
16 for though the righteous fall seven times, they rise again,
    but the wicked stumble when calamity strikes.

*Saying 28*

17 Do not gloat when your enemy falls;
    when they stumble, do not let your heart rejoice,
18 or the Lord will see and disapprove
    and turn his wrath away from them.

*Saying 29*

19 Do not fret because of evildoers
    or be envious of the wicked,
20 for the evildoer has no future hope,
    and the lamp of the wicked will be snuffed out.

*Saying 30*

21 Fear the Lord and the king, my son,
    and do not join with rebellious officials,
22 for those two will send sudden destruction on them,
    and who knows what calamities they can bring?

## Further Sayings of the Wise

²³These also are sayings of the wise:

To show partiality in judging is not good:
²⁴Whoever says to the guilty, "You are innocent,"
　　will be cursed by peoples and denounced by nations.
²⁵But it will go well with those who convict the guilty,
　　and rich blessing will come on them.

²⁶An honest answer
　　is like a kiss on the lips.

²⁷Put your outdoor work in order
　　and get your fields ready;
　　after that, build your house.

²⁸Do not testify against your neighbor without cause—
　　would you use your lips to mislead?
²⁹Do not say, "I'll do to them as they have done to me;
　　I'll pay them back for what they did."

³⁰I went past the field of a sluggard,
　　past the vineyard of someone who has no sense;
³¹thorns had come up everywhere,
　　the ground was covered with weeds,
　　and the stone wall was in ruins.
³²I applied my heart to what I observed
　　and learned a lesson from what I saw:
³³A little sleep, a little slumber,
　　a little folding of the hands to rest—
³⁴and poverty will come on you like a thief
　　and scarcity like an armed man.

## More Proverbs of Solomon

**25** These are more proverbs of Solomon, compiled by the men of Hezekiah king of Judah:

²It is the glory of God to conceal a matter;
　　to search out a matter is the glory of kings.
³As the heavens are high and the earth is deep,
　　so the hearts of kings are unsearchable.

⁴Remove the dross from the silver,
　　and a silversmith can produce a vessel;
⁵remove wicked officials from the king's presence,
　　and his throne will be established through righteousness.

⁶Do not exalt yourself in the king's presence,
　　and do not claim a place among his great men;
⁷it is better for him to say to you, "Come up here,"
　　than for him to humiliate you before his nobles.

What you have seen with your eyes
⁸　do not bring*ᵃ* hastily to court,
for what will you do in the end
　　if your neighbor puts you to shame?

---

*ᵃ7,8 Or nobles / on whom you had set your eyes. / ⁸Do not go*

⁹ If you take your neighbor to court,
 do not betray another's confidence,
¹⁰ or the one who hears it may shame you
 and the charge against you will stand.

¹¹ Like apples[a] of gold in settings of silver
 is a ruling rightly given.
¹² Like an earring of gold or an ornament of fine gold
 is the rebuke of a wise judge to a listening ear.

¹³ Like a snow-cooled drink at harvest time
 is a trustworthy messenger to the one who sends him;
 he refreshes the spirit of his master.
¹⁴ Like clouds and wind without rain
 is one who boasts of gifts never given.

¹⁵ Through patience a ruler can be persuaded,
 and a gentle tongue can break a bone.

¹⁶ If you find honey, eat just enough —
 too much of it, and you will vomit.
¹⁷ Seldom set foot in your neighbor's house —
 too much of you, and they will hate you.

¹⁸ Like a club or a sword or a sharp arrow
 is one who gives false testimony against a neighbor.
¹⁹ Like a broken tooth or a lame foot
 is reliance on the unfaithful in a time of trouble.
²⁰ Like one who takes away a garment on a cold day,
 or like vinegar poured on a wound,
 is one who sings songs to a heavy heart.

²¹ If your enemy is hungry, give him food to eat;
 if he is thirsty, give him water to drink.
²² In doing this, you will heap burning coals on his head,
 and the LORD will reward you.

²³ Like a north wind that brings unexpected rain
 is a sly tongue — which provokes a horrified look.

²⁴ Better to live on a corner of the roof
 than share a house with a quarrelsome wife.

²⁵ Like cold water to a weary soul
 is good news from a distant land.
²⁶ Like a muddied spring or a polluted well
 are the righteous who give way to the wicked.

²⁷ It is not good to eat too much honey,
 nor is it honorable to search out matters that are
  too deep.

²⁸ Like a city whose walls are broken through
 is a person who lacks self-control.

**26** Like snow in summer or rain in harvest,
 honor is not fitting for a fool.
² Like a fluttering sparrow or a darting swallow,
 an undeserved curse does not come to rest.

---

[a] 11 Or possibly *apricots*

Like Apples of Gold in Settings of Silver is a Ruling Rightly Given.

PROVERBS 25:11

³ A whip for the horse, a bridle for the donkey,
    and a rod for the backs of fools!
⁴ Do not answer a fool according to his folly,
    or you yourself will be just like him.
⁵ Answer a fool according to his folly,
    or he will be wise in his own eyes.
⁶ Sending a message by the hands of a fool
    is like cutting off one's feet or drinking poison.
⁷ Like the useless legs of one who is lame
    is a proverb in the mouth of a fool.
⁸ Like tying a stone in a sling
    is the giving of honor to a fool.
⁹ Like a thornbush in a drunkard's hand
    is a proverb in the mouth of a fool.
¹⁰ Like an archer who wounds at random
    is one who hires a fool or any passer-by.
¹¹ As a dog returns to its vomit,
    so fools repeat their folly.
¹² Do you see a person wise in their own eyes?
    There is more hope for a fool than for them.

¹³ A sluggard says, "There's a lion in the road,
    a fierce lion roaming the streets!"
¹⁴ As a door turns on its hinges,
    so a sluggard turns on his bed.
¹⁵ A sluggard buries his hand in the dish;
    he is too lazy to bring it back to his mouth.
¹⁶ A sluggard is wiser in his own eyes
    than seven people who answer discreetly.

¹⁷ Like one who grabs a stray dog by the ears
    is someone who rushes into a quarrel not their own.

¹⁸ Like a maniac shooting
    flaming arrows of death
¹⁹ is one who deceives their neighbor
    and says, "I was only joking!"

²⁰ Without wood a fire goes out;
    without a gossip a quarrel dies down.
²¹ As charcoal to embers and as wood to fire,
    so is a quarrelsome person for kindling strife.
²² The words of a gossip are like choice morsels;
    they go down to the inmost parts.

²³ Like a coating of silver dross on earthenware
    are fervent[a] lips with an evil heart.
²⁴ Enemies disguise themselves with their lips,
    but in their hearts they harbor deceit.
²⁵ Though their speech is charming, do not believe them,
    for seven abominations fill their hearts.
²⁶ Their malice may be concealed by deception,
    but their wickedness will be exposed in the assembly.
²⁷ Whoever digs a pit will fall into it;
    if someone rolls a stone, it will roll back on them.

---

[a] 23 Hebrew; Septuagint *smooth*

²⁸ A lying tongue hates those it hurts,
and a flattering mouth works ruin.

**27** Do not boast about tomorrow,
for you do not know what a day may bring.

² Let someone else praise you, and not your own mouth;
an outsider, and not your own lips.

³ Stone is heavy and sand a burden,
but a fool's provocation is heavier than both.

⁴ Anger is cruel and fury overwhelming,
but who can stand before jealousy?

⁵ Better is open rebuke
than hidden love.

⁶ Wounds from a friend can be trusted,
but an enemy multiplies kisses.

⁷ One who is full loathes honey from the comb,
but to the hungry even what is bitter tastes sweet.

⁸ Like a bird that flees its nest
is anyone who flees from home.

⁹ Perfume and incense bring joy to the heart,
and the pleasantness of a friend
springs from their heartfelt advice.

¹⁰ Do not forsake your friend or a friend of your family,
and do not go to your relative's house when disaster
strikes you —
better a neighbor nearby than a relative far away.

¹¹ Be wise, my son, and bring joy to my heart;
then I can answer anyone who treats me with contempt.

¹² The prudent see danger and take refuge,
but the simple keep going and pay the penalty.

¹³ Take the garment of one who puts up security for a stranger;
hold it in pledge if it is done for an outsider.

¹⁴ If anyone loudly blesses their neighbor early in the
morning,
it will be taken as a curse.

¹⁵ A quarrelsome wife is like the dripping
of a leaky roof in a rainstorm;
¹⁶ restraining her is like restraining the wind
or grasping oil with the hand.

¹⁷ As iron sharpens iron,
so one person sharpens another.

¹⁸ The one who guards a fig tree will eat its fruit,
and whoever protects their master will be honored.

¹⁹ As water reflects the face,
so one's life reflects the heart.ᵃ

---

ᵃ 19 Or *so others reflect your heart back to you*

AS IRON SHARPENS IRON, SO ONE PERSON SHARPENS ANOTHER.

PROVERBS 27:17

20 Death and Destruction[a] are never satisfied,
 and neither are human eyes.

21 The crucible for silver and the furnace for gold,
 but people are tested by their praise.

22 Though you grind a fool in a mortar,
 grinding them like grain with a pestle,
 you will not remove their folly from them.

23 Be sure you know the condition of your flocks,
 give careful attention to your herds;
24 for riches do not endure forever,
 and a crown is not secure for all generations.
25 When the hay is removed and new growth appears
 and the grass from the hills is gathered in,
26 the lambs will provide you with clothing,
 and the goats with the price of a field.
27 You will have plenty of goats' milk to feed your family
 and to nourish your female servants.

28 The wicked flee though no one pursues,
 but the righteous are as bold as a lion.

2 When a country is rebellious, it has many rulers,
 but a ruler with discernment and knowledge maintains order.

3 A ruler[b] who oppresses the poor
 is like a driving rain that leaves no crops.

4 Those who forsake instruction praise the wicked,
 but those who heed it resist them.

5 Evildoers do not understand what is right,
 but those who seek the LORD understand it fully.

6 Better the poor whose walk is blameless
 than the rich whose ways are perverse.

7 A discerning son heeds instruction,
 but a companion of gluttons disgraces his father.

8 Whoever increases wealth by taking interest or profit from
 the poor
 amasses it for another, who will be kind to the poor.

9 If anyone turns a deaf ear to my instruction,
 even their prayers are detestable.

10 Whoever leads the upright along an evil path
 will fall into their own trap,
 but the blameless will receive a good inheritance.

11 The rich are wise in their own eyes;
 one who is poor and discerning sees how deluded they are.

12 When the righteous triumph, there is great elation;
 but when the wicked rise to power, people go into hiding.

13 Whoever conceals their sins does not prosper,
 but the one who confesses and renounces them finds mercy.

---

[a] 20 Hebrew *Abaddon*    [b] 3 Or *A poor person*

¹⁴ Blessed is the one who always trembles before God,
   but whoever hardens their heart falls into trouble.

¹⁵ Like a roaring lion or a charging bear
   is a wicked ruler over a helpless people.

¹⁶ A tyrannical ruler practices extortion,
   but one who hates ill-gotten gain will enjoy a long reign.

¹⁷ Anyone tormented by the guilt of murder
   will seek refuge in the grave;
   let no one hold them back.

¹⁸ The one whose walk is blameless is kept safe,
   but the one whose ways are perverse will fall into the pit.ᵃ

¹⁹ Those who work their land will have abundant food,
   but those who chase fantasies will have their fill of poverty.

²⁰ A faithful person will be richly blessed,
   but one eager to get rich will not go unpunished.

²¹ To show partiality is not good —
   yet a person will do wrong for a piece of bread.

²² The stingy are eager to get rich
   and are unaware that poverty awaits them.

²³ Whoever rebukes a person will in the end gain favor
   rather than one who has a flattering tongue.

²⁴ Whoever robs their father or mother
   and says, "It's not wrong,"
   is partner to one who destroys.

²⁵ The greedy stir up conflict,
   but those who trust in the Lord will prosper.

²⁶ Those who trust in themselves are fools,
   but those who walk in wisdom are kept safe.

²⁷ Those who give to the poor will lack nothing,
   but those who close their eyes to them receive many
       curses.

²⁸ When the wicked rise to power, people go into hiding;
   but when the wicked perish, the righteous thrive.

**29** Whoever remains stiff-necked after many rebukes
   will suddenly be destroyed — without remedy.

² When the righteous thrive, the people rejoice;
   when the wicked rule, the people groan.

³ A man who loves wisdom brings joy to his father,
   but a companion of prostitutes squanders his wealth.

⁴ By justice a king gives a country stability,
   but those who are greedy forᵇ bribes tear it down.

⁵ Those who flatter their neighbors
   are spreading nets for their feet.

---

ᵃ 18 Syriac (see Septuagint); Hebrew *into one*    ᵇ 4 Or *who give*

⁶Evildoers are snared by their own sin,
but the righteous shout for joy and are glad.

⁷The righteous care about justice for the poor,
but the wicked have no such concern.

⁸Mockers stir up a city,
but the wise turn away anger.

⁹If a wise person goes to court with a fool,
the fool rages and scoffs, and there is no peace.

¹⁰The bloodthirsty hate a person of integrity
and seek to kill the upright.

¹¹Fools give full vent to their rage,
but the wise bring calm in the end.

¹²If a ruler listens to lies,
all his officials become wicked.

¹³The poor and the oppressor have this in common:
The LORD gives sight to the eyes of both.

¹⁴If a king judges the poor with fairness,
his throne will be established forever.

¹⁵A rod and a reprimand impart wisdom,
but a child left undisciplined disgraces its mother.

¹⁶When the wicked thrive, so does sin,
but the righteous will see their downfall.

¹⁷Discipline your children, and they will give you peace;
they will bring you the delights you desire.

¹⁸Where there is no revelation, people cast off restraint;
but blessed is the one who heeds wisdom's instruction.

¹⁹Servants cannot be corrected by mere words;
though they understand, they will not respond.

²⁰Do you see someone who speaks in haste?
There is more hope for a fool than for them.

²¹A servant pampered from youth
will turn out to be insolent.

²²An angry person stirs up conflict,
and a hot-tempered person commits many sins.

²³Pride brings a person low,
but the lowly in spirit gain honor.

²⁴The accomplices of thieves are their own enemies;
they are put under oath and dare not testify.

²⁵Fear of man will prove to be a snare,
but whoever trusts in the LORD is kept safe.

²⁶Many seek an audience with a ruler,
but it is from the LORD that one gets justice.

²⁷The righteous detest the dishonest;
the wicked detest the upright.

## Sayings of Agur

**30** The sayings of Agur son of Jakeh — an inspired utterance.

This man's utterance to Ithiel:

"I am weary, God,
    but I can prevail.*ᵃ*
² Surely I am only a brute, not a man;
    I do not have human understanding.
³ I have not learned wisdom,
    nor have I attained to the knowledge of the Holy One.
⁴ Who has gone up to heaven and come down?
    Whose hands have gathered up the wind?
Who has wrapped up the waters in a cloak?
    Who has established all the ends of the earth?
What is his name, and what is the name of his son?
    Surely you know!

⁵ "Every word of God is flawless;
    he is a shield to those who take refuge in him.
⁶ Do not add to his words,
    or he will rebuke you and prove you a liar.

⁷ "Two things I ask of you, LORD;
    do not refuse me before I die:
⁸ Keep falsehood and lies far from me;
    give me neither poverty nor riches,
    but give me only my daily bread.
⁹ Otherwise, I may have too much and disown you
    and say, 'Who is the LORD?'
Or I may become poor and steal,
    and so dishonor the name of my God.

¹⁰ "Do not slander a servant to their master,
    or they will curse you, and you will pay for it.

¹¹ "There are those who curse their fathers
    and do not bless their mothers;
¹² those who are pure in their own eyes
    and yet are not cleansed of their filth;
¹³ those whose eyes are ever so haughty,
    whose glances are so disdainful;
¹⁴ those whose teeth are swords
    and whose jaws are set with knives
to devour the poor from the earth
    and the needy from among mankind.

¹⁵ "The leech has two daughters.
    'Give! Give!' they cry.

"There are three things that are never satisfied,
    four that never say, 'Enough!':
¹⁶ the grave, the barren womb,
    land, which is never satisfied with water,
    and fire, which never says, 'Enough!'

---

*ᵃ 1* With a different word division of the Hebrew; Masoretic Text *utterance to Ithiel, / to Ithiel and Ukal:*

EVERY *word* OF GOD - is - FLAWLESS.

PROVERBS
30:5

¹⁷ "The eye that mocks a father,
    that scorns an aged mother,
  will be pecked out by the ravens of the valley,
    will be eaten by the vultures.

¹⁸ "There are three things that are too amazing for me,
    four that I do not understand:
¹⁹ the way of an eagle in the sky,
    the way of a snake on a rock,
  the way of a ship on the high seas,
    and the way of a man with a young woman.

²⁰ "This is the way of an adulterous woman:
    She eats and wipes her mouth
    and says, 'I've done nothing wrong.'

²¹ "Under three things the earth trembles,
    under four it cannot bear up:
²² a servant who becomes king,
    a godless fool who gets plenty to eat,
²³ a contemptible woman who gets married,
    and a servant who displaces her mistress.

²⁴ "Four things on earth are small,
    yet they are extremely wise:
²⁵ Ants are creatures of little strength,
    yet they store up their food in the summer;
²⁶ hyraxes are creatures of little power,
    yet they make their home in the crags;
²⁷ locusts have no king,
    yet they advance together in ranks;
²⁸ a lizard can be caught with the hand,
    yet it is found in kings' palaces.

²⁹ "There are three things that are stately in their stride,
    four that move with stately bearing:
³⁰ a lion, mighty among beasts,
    who retreats before nothing;
³¹ a strutting rooster, a he-goat,
    and a king secure against revolt.ᵃ

³² "If you play the fool and exalt yourself,
    or if you plan evil,
    clap your hand over your mouth!
³³ For as churning cream produces butter,
    and as twisting the nose produces blood,
    so stirring up anger produces strife."

## Sayings of King Lemuel

**31** The sayings of King Lemuel — an inspired utterance his mother taught him.

² Listen, my son! Listen, son of my womb!
    Listen, my son, the answer to my prayers!
³ Do not spend your strengthᵇ on women,
    your vigor on those who ruin kings.

---

ᵃ 31 The meaning of the Hebrew for this phrase is uncertain.    ᵇ 3 Or *wealth*

⁴It is not for kings, Lemuel —
 it is not for kings to drink wine,
 not for rulers to crave beer,
⁵lest they drink and forget what has been decreed,
 and deprive all the oppressed of their rights.
⁶Let beer be for those who are perishing,
 wine for those who are in anguish!
⁷Let them drink and forget their poverty
 and remember their misery no more.

⁸Speak up for those who cannot speak for themselves,
 for the rights of all who are destitute.
⁹Speak up and judge fairly;
 defend the rights of the poor and needy.

## Epilogue: The Wife of Noble Character

¹⁰ ᵃA wife of noble character who can find?
 She is worth far more than rubies.
¹¹Her husband has full confidence in her
 and lacks nothing of value.
¹²She brings him good, not harm,
 all the days of her life.
¹³She selects wool and flax
 and works with eager hands.
¹⁴She is like the merchant ships,
 bringing her food from afar.
¹⁵She gets up while it is still night;
 she provides food for her family
 and portions for her female servants.
¹⁶She considers a field and buys it;
 out of her earnings she plants a vineyard.
¹⁷She sets about her work vigorously;
 her arms are strong for her tasks.
¹⁸She sees that her trading is profitable,
 and her lamp does not go out at night.
¹⁹In her hand she holds the distaff
 and grasps the spindle with her fingers.
²⁰She opens her arms to the poor
 and extends her hands to the needy.
²¹When it snows, she has no fear for her household;
 for all of them are clothed in scarlet.
²²She makes coverings for her bed;
 she is clothed in fine linen and purple.
²³Her husband is respected at the city gate,
 where he takes his seat among the elders of the land.
²⁴She makes linen garments and sells them,
 and supplies the merchants with sashes.
²⁵She is clothed with strength and dignity;
 she can laugh at the days to come.
²⁶She speaks with wisdom,
 and faithful instruction is on her tongue.

---

ᵃ 10 Verses 10-31 are an acrostic poem, the verses of which begin with the successive letters of the Hebrew alphabet.

<sup>27</sup> She watches over the affairs of her household
    and does not eat the bread of idleness.
<sup>28</sup> Her children arise and call her blessed;
    her husband also, and he praises her:
<sup>29</sup> "Many women do noble things,
    but you surpass them all."
<sup>30</sup> Charm is deceptive, and beauty is fleeting;
    but a woman who fears the LORD is to be praised.
<sup>31</sup> Honor her for all that her hands have done,
    and let her works bring her praise at the city gate.

Charm is deceptive, & Beauty is fleeting; but a woman who fears the LORD is to be praised.

PROVERBS 31:30

# Table of Weights and Measures

|  | Biblical Unit | Approximate American Equivalent | | Approximate Metric Equivalent | |
|---|---|---|---|---|---|
| **Weights** | talent (60 minas) | 75 | pounds | 34 | kilograms |
|  | mina (50 shekels) | 1 1/4 | pounds | 560 | grams |
|  | shekel (2 bekas) | 2/5 | ounce | 11.5 | grams |
|  | pim (2/3 shekel) | 1/4 | ounce | 7.8 | grams |
|  | beka (10 gerahs) | 1/5 | ounce | 5.7 | grams |
|  | gerah | 1/50 | ounce | 0.6 | gram |
|  | daric | 1/3 | ounce | 8.4 | grams |
| **Length** | cubit | 18 | inches | 45 | centimeters |
|  | span | 9 | inches | 23 | centimeters |
|  | handbreadth | 3 | inches | 7.5 | centimeters |
|  | stadion (pl. stadia) | 600 | feet | 183 | meters |
| **Capacity** *Dry Measure* | cor [homer] (10 ephahs) | 6 | bushels | 220 | liters |
|  | lethek (5 ephahs) | 3 | bushels | 110 | liters |
|  | ephah (10 omers) | 3/5 | bushel | 22 | liters |
|  | seah (1/3 ephah) | 7 | quarts | 7.5 | liters |
|  | omer (1/10 ephah) | 2 | quarts | 2 | liters |
|  | cab (1/18 ephah) | 1 | quart | 1 | liter |
| *Liquid Measure* | bath (1 ephah) | 6 | gallons | 22 | liters |
|  | hin (1/6 bath) | 1 | gallon | 3.8 | liters |
|  | log (1/72 bath) | 1/3 | quart | 0.3 | liter |

The figures of the table are calculated on the basis of a shekel equaling 11.5 grams, a cubit equaling 18 inches and an ephah equaling 22 liters. The quart referred to is either a dry quart (slightly larger than a liter) or a liquid quart (slightly smaller than a liter), whichever is applicable. The ton referred to in the footnotes is the American ton of 2,000 pounds. These weights are calculated relative to the particular commodity involved. Accordingly, the same measure of capacity in the text may be converted into different weights in the footnotes.

This table is based upon the best available information, but it is not intended to be mathematically precise; like the measurement equivalents in the footnotes, it merely gives approximate amounts and distances. Weights and measures differed somewhat at various times and places in the ancient world. There is uncertainty particularly about the ephah and the bath; further discoveries may shed more light on these units of capacity.

# Index of Artists and Their Work

# Notes

# Notes

# Notes

# Notes

# Notes

# Notes

# Notes

# Notes

# Notes

# Notes

## A NOTE REGARDING THE TYPE

This Bible was set in the Zondervan NIV Typeface, commissioned by Zondervan, a division of HarperCollins Christian Publishing, and designed in Aarhus, Denmark, by Klaus E. Krogh and Heidi Rand Sørensen of 2K/DENMARK. The design takes inspiration from the vision of the New International Version (NIV) to be a modern translation that gives the reader the most accurate Bible text possible, reflects the very best of biblical scholarship, and uses contemporary global English. The designers of the Zondervan NIV Typeface sought to reflect this rich, half-century-old tradition of accuracy, readability, and clarity while also embodying the best advancements in modern Bible typography. The result is a distinctive, open Bible typeface that is uncompromisingly beautiful, clear, readable at any size, and perfectly suited to the New International Version.